The Bridge Called Grief

Blue Cliff Monastery
3 Mindfulness Road
Pine Bush, NY 12566

The Bridge Called Grief

Mary Kate Jordan

Book design by Jessika Hazelton

Printed in the United States of America

The Troy Book Makers • Troy, New York • thetroybookmakers.com

To order additional copies of this title,
contact your favorite local bookstore
or visit www.tbmbooks.com

ISBN: 978-1-61468-082-6

for all who walk the bridge called grief

for Storrs and Shirley Olds
in memory of Anson

*The risk of love is loss,
and the price of love is grief.*

– Hilary Stanton Zunin

Since no book is ever written in a vacuum,
I owe warm thanks to too many people to mention here.
All your names are written on my heart, especially
Bonsai Cox,
Alecz Adams, Deirdre Breen, Nancy Claiborne, Julie Michaels,
Belinda Owen, Diane Plourde, Katharine Rossi,
Claudette Webster, JoAnne Webster,
Pam Weeks, and Eric Wilska.

Once upon a time,
Peace was a harbor
where you could safely anchor.

But that was before.

Before your loss.

Before you took your first steps toward
the bridge called grief.

Grief is a bridge across a great emptiness,

an emptiness so wide
you may feel
no one has ever been in this exact place before,
or felt your specific pain.

And no one ever has.

Grief
is a turned-down smile,
a mass of stone in your chest
that surrounds your beating heart.

As you first step onto this bridge,
you might feel your dreams
and goals for the future
slide away
like running water.

Even though one end of the bridge
is rooted in yesterday, and
the other end is rooted in tomorrow,
often you can only see the spot
right where you are standing,

Today is the place in time where
you just
keep
putting
one foot
in front of
the other.

It is the time when you learn
what the Buddha taught:
The greatest prayer is patience.

Grief has an inner logic all its own that is different from the way your everyday mind thinks, plans, and decides.

On this bridge, sometimes
everything seems
dark as night.

Once in a while, you notice that
the moon comes out.

Other times,
you just want to
curl up and hide for a while.

Some days, you might feel like
the bridge itself is under water
and there's nothing to do but
walk along the rocky shore
feeling awful, broken, lost.

On other days, you might pick up some little thing that
catches your eye along the water's edge:

a seashell,

a stone,

a piece of driftwood.

You might throw your treasure
far out to sea.
Or you might stash it in your pocket,
and start to make a collection.

But as you walk along, finding, tossing,
collecting,
you may feel the bridge called grief
under your feet once more.

Strange as it seems,
and no matter what yours looks like,
the bridge itself is
your most dependable place to be right now.

One of your most difficult tasks is to navigate the hard changes your loss requires.

The way ahead can look rough and empty.
You do not know if you will have the strength,
let alone how you will do it.

It is not a journey you must complete today.

But as you take one step at a time,

or, as you stand still for a while and wait,

the details
of the landscape you see
will start to change.

Things may seem
the same drab gray,
but the fog will start to lift.

And, yes, the fog comes in again.
Lifts again.
In and out.

But as you move along the bridge,
bit by bit
you will become more aware of
the wider world around you.

Still, be gentle with yourself.

You may think
you do not have the tools you need to recover,
and that the work is futile.

But you do,

or you will,

and it is not.

Grief has its own strange clock,
and its own calendar.

Living in this time warp
can feel crazy-making, and
grieving takes time.

Sometimes change emerges gradually,
like the end of a long, cold winter.

Sometimes, change
is right at your fingertips.
Sometimes just reaching out
is the change.

Either way,

change

happens.

Even as your grief changes shape,
your journey is still trustworthy.

Every time the bridge called grief points south,
the weather begins to warm.

Whenever the bridge points west,
the fog continues to clear.

The authority of grief begins to fade.

When the bridge
points north,
it can be
hard
to find
your way.

But, soon,
the light starts to
dance with the snow and
a path appears.

And there are days when
the bridge turns east.

Suddenly, you find yourself
face to face
with a beautiful dawn.

Eventually,
grief will lead you
to a new entrance
into that once-familiar country called
Peace.

Peace will open,
wide and beautiful before you.

You might run right in.

Or you might reel back in shock.

You might refuse
to step down from the bridge at all.

You might hate Peace for feeling so inviting.
How could you leave the bridge
that connects you
to all you have lost?

Maybe you will decide to

stand still

for a while

and

just

look

back.

Or you might go ahead and
step into Peace…
but
very, very,
cautiously.

Maybe it's OK to visit Peace,
but only on Mondays.

Or you can see the sights,
but only through the tour bus windows.

Then you will make your way back to the
bridge that brought you here.

This bridge is a lonely stretch of highway.

But you know where you are,
and it knows where you have been.

This bridge connects back to
all you have lost.
On it, grief has felt like a reliable companion.

As it should be,
for a while.

This bridge has cradled your pain.

But it also leads you to Peace,
though it would never make you live there
before you are ready.

When you decide to
go ahead and explore
what the place has to offer,
do not fly too high,
too far,
or too soon.

Like every experience,
your walk on the bridge called grief
has an impact on you.
Sometimes you feel lighter, hopeful.
From time to time, you feel numb.
Other times you feel tense,
angry, sad, or sleepy.
This shift is natural, like breathing
but it is also hard work.

Tears are the silent language of grief, according to Voltaire, and you cannot tell when you might just collapse like a heap of stones.

Sometimes a heap of stones is a good thing to be.

It might be a memorial,

a threshold,

even a doorway.

What if, one day, you find
you have stayed in the country called Peace
all day?

You might feel wonderful about that.

Most likely you will feel both
wonderful and guilty,

until one day you realize
the familiar bridge is no longer
a magnet under your feet.

You are starting to feel like
you've moved into a new home.

You are at Peace.

Coming to Peace
takes courage.

Moving into Peace
only comes at the end of an epic journey.

It is a safari into the broken heart of life.

You are both the traveler and the witness.

On this journey,
you discover that
leaving the bridge called grief
is not abandoning your love,
or denying your loss.

Reaching the far end of the bridge is
different from reaching the end of pain.
It is reaching
higher ground.

You arrive at a spot where you can see clearly,
a place where your loss,
your love,
and your life
are all honored.

Even though each of us
walks our bridge of grief alone,
it is good to know
others have walked it, too.

Others who have learned
to live in the new land;

others who want you to
know that living here is possible.

It is good to know that, even now,
you might be able to
hear them
whisper,

Welcome.